GRANNY'S LOST HER MARBLES

GRANNY'S LOST HER MARBLES

Robert Eringer

Illustrated by
James Harper

LONDON

Published by:

Bedlam Books
13 Heath Street
London, NW3 6TP
Great Britain

In collaboration with:

Bartleby Press
11141 Georgia Avenue
Silver Spring, MD 20902
USA

ISBN: 0-910155-52-6
Printed in China

Granny was not feeling well one morning.

She did not have a sore throat.

She did not have a headache.

Granny did not have an upset tummy.

Something was
unwell with
Granny's brain.

Granny did not
know her brain
was unwell.

Other family members recognized that something about Granny was not right.

It began like this:

Granny announced that strangers were watching her.

Nobody in the family paid much attention to what Granny said, even though they all lived in the same house.

(Gramps had already gone to heaven.)

Maybe strangers *were* watching Granny.

Who cared?

Granny cared, that's who.

And maybe that was part of the problem.

Granny's family did not give her much attention.

So Granny got worse.

Strangers were not just watching her any more, said Granny.

Strangers wanted to *hurt* her.

Why would anyone want to hurt Granny?

Granny believed she knew the reason.

But she would not tell anyone in her family the reason.

It was secret, said Granny.

Still, nobody in the family paid Granny much attention.

If anything, they thought Granny's new ideas were amusing.

But it soon got worse.

Granny said the strangers (thirty-two, she had counted) were trying to *kill* her.

Someone in the family asked, Who would want to kill *you*, Granny?

Granny just nodded, with a mad look in her eyes.

Someone in the family asked Granny *how* all these strangers were trying to kill her.

All Granny would
say was that
they, the
strangers, were
directing
dangerous rays,
from streetlamps,
into her bedroom.

To stop these light rays getting in, Granny filled her window curtains with thousands of pins and needles.

Granny stayed in her bedroom all day, every day.

She would not join her family for breakfast, tea, or dinner.

Granny's family placed food outside her door at meal times.

But Granny would not eat any of the food served to her.

She thought
these meals
were poisoned.

Instead, Granny tiptoed to the kitchen in the middle of the night to look for packaged food, like crackers or crisps, which had not yet been opened.

After eating, Granny would pace up and down the hallway, muttering, as her family tried to sleep.

Granny had lost her marbles.

Granny's ideas were not amusing any more.

What if Granny tired to hurt someone?

(On one late-night visit to the kitchen, Granny switched on the gas jets and left them running.

It might have caused a nasty explosion.)

So Granny's family called the doctor and told him Granny had lost her marbles.

The doctor came to the house to see Granny for himself.

Granny came out
to see who was
there.

But when she saw
the doctor,
Granny spun
around and made
a beeline for her
bedroom.

The doctor and his assistants caught Granny and stopped her running away.

They put Granny into their car and drove her to a special hospital for people with unwell brains.

A special doctor, called a *psychiatrist*, listened to Granny say that her family was trying to kill her with electric light-beams from streetlamps.

The special doctor decided that Granny had a brain problem called *paranoid-schizophrenia*.

These big fancy words meant that Granny heard voices that told her untrue things.

These voices were imaginary, but Granny thought they were real.

The special doctor wanted Granny to stay at his hospital for a few weeks so he could watch her.

Granny did not want to stay at the special hospital and be watched.

But Granny had to stay.

Sometimes, when people cannot take care of themselves, or if they become a danger to their families, they must do what the special doctor says.

So Granny stayed at the hospital, in a special section called a mental ward.

Granny shared a room with a black woman who also heard voices.

The black woman carried a little doll named Voodoo.

She pierced her doll with pins that she hid from the special doctor and his nurses.

Granny made a few new friends.

One of Granny's friends liked to take off all her clothes and run around naked.

Another of Granny's friends talked to herself a lot.

This friend heard voices just like Granny, and she liked to yell back at the voices.

The special doctor gave Granny some special medicine.

The medicine helped Granny relax. But she still heard voices.

After a few weeks of medicine, the special doctor decided that Granny needed electro-shock therapy.

Electro-shock treatment was scary for Granny.

For a long time before she came to the special hospital, Granny believed strange people wanted to fill her body with electricity.

Now this special
doctor and his
nurses, who were
strangers to
Granny, wanted to
fill her body with
electricity.

The special
doctor believed
he could shock
Granny's brain
back to normal.

He and his nurses
strapped Granny
to a bed on wheels
and rolled her into
the electro-shock
therapy room.

Big Nurse pushed
a mouth-guard
onto Granny's
teeth so she could
not bite her own
tongue.

Another nurse planted wires onto Granny's head.

The special doctor pressed a button.

Granny was jolted by lots and lots of electricity.

When Granny awakened, she did not think strange people were watching her.

She did not think her family was trying to kill her with light rays from streetlamps.

And she did not
hear voices any
more. Granny's
marbles had
returned. Most of
them, anyway.

When Granny came home, she could not remember things as well as she once did.

Granny had to take
special pills that
made her burp a
lot.

And Granny
thought the family
dog was a cat.

But now Granny
was harmless.